NETWORKS

ISLAND TREASURES

John McInnes, *Senior Author*
Clayton Graves
Christine McClymont

NELSON CANADA

© Nelson Canada,
A Division of International Thomson Limited, 1988

All rights in this book are reserved

Published in 1988 by
Nelson Canada,
A Division of International Thomson Limited
1120 Birchmount Road
Scarborough, Ontario
M1K 5G4

ISBN 0-17-602507-3

Canadian Cataloguing in Publication Data

Main entry under title:

Island Treasures

(Networks)

ISBN 0-17-602507-3

1. Readers (Primary).   I. McInnes, John, 1927-
II. Graves, Clayton.   III. McClymont,
Christine.   IV. Series: Networks (Toronto, Ont.).

PE1119.I84 1987   428.6   C87-094576-9

Printed and bound in Canada

Contents

Better Together

Because we do all things together,
All things improve, even weather.

Hockey Stuck

by *Ted Staunton*

It was the old glop trick. I fell for it every time. Chocolate glop was my favourite dessert—ice cream, chocolate sauce, and bananas all mushed together. We only had it after I'd been really good. Or before I had to do something I really didn't like. My mom figured I'd be so happy about the glop, I wouldn't mind as much.

"It's time for Saturday classes at the community school again," Mom announced. "What do you want to take this fall, Cyril?"

"Nothing," I said, as fast as I could. Now I knew why I was having chocolate glop. I hated Saturday classes. Everybody but me always seemed to know everybody else. I was the only one who was never any good at what we were doing.

"You can meet new friends," said my dad, "and learn something new. There's lots to choose from."

"I don't like doing any of that stuff," I said.

"You haven't heard what there is yet." My dad read from the list in the booklet, "There's judo, crafts, floor hockey, baton, piano, and gymnastics."

"Yuck," I said.

"Cyril," said my dad. He read the list again. Maybe there was one I liked after all.

"Piano," I said.

"You can't take that, dear," said my mom. "We don't have a piano."

"How about floor hockey?" asked my dad.

I knew what that meant—getting picked last, never getting a pass, getting pushed around by the big guys.

"Yuck," I said.

"Give it a try. I'll bet it's fun," said my mom.

"It'll be good for you," said my dad.

"Awwwwww," I said.

"Eat your glop, dear," they said.

I did, but it didn't taste as good anymore.

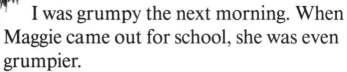

I was grumpy the next morning. When Maggie came out for school, she was even grumpier.

"Cyril," she said. "The most terrible thing that ever happened to me has happened. I have to take piano lessons." She booted a stone down the street.

"You think that's bad?" I said. "I have to take floor hockey."

"Ever lucky!" said Maggie. "That's what I wanted."

"Am not," I said. "I wanted piano."

We walked a little farther and Maggie said, "Why don't we trade? You take piano for me, and I'll play floor hockey for you."

"How can we do that?" I asked.

"Easy. We'll just switch places. Nobody will know. You can sneak over and use the piano in our basement, and I can play all the hockey I want." Maggie got all excited making plans as we walked down Greenapple Street.

"We'll get in trouble," I said.

"Come on, Cyril," Maggie said. "Partners help each other, right? And we're partners."

"Yes, but..." I began.

"I bet Ugly Augie Crumley signs up for floor hockey."

"Okay, let's trade," I said.

And that's what we did. The first Saturday morning, I told the piano teacher that "Maggie" was supposed to be "Maxie." Maggie told the floor hockey instructor that "Cyril" was supposed to be "Cheryl." Nobody told on me because none of my friends took piano. Nobody told on Maggie because all the kids wanted her on their team.

When it was time to go home, I gave Maggie her piano book. She gave me my running shoes.

"Thanks to me," she said, "you got four goals and three assists. What a star! Your parents won't believe it. What did I learn?"

"Where to find middle C, how to hold your fingers, and a song called 'Up and Down.' It has three notes and I—I mean you—can almost play it already."

I was so proud of myself that I wanted to start playing Maggie's piano right away. After lunch, I snuck over to Maggie's. She let me in the side door and we slipped down into the basement.

"I'm practising now, so start timing," she yelled upstairs. Then she closed the door. "Play loud," said Maggie. "I said I was nervous so my parents promised not to look, but they'll be listening for sure. And make it good. It's supposed to be a genius playing the piano, remember?" She flopped on the sofa and opened a book.

I sat down at the piano. It was a lot nicer and newer than the one at school. The wood smelled fresh and a little mysterious—like a treasure chest would smell. The keys gleamed black and white. They were so clean that I didn't want to touch them at first.

Softly I pressed a key. It sank under my finger, and a note boomed out loud enough to blow the house down. Nobody seemed to notice. I put my fingers in the right place and tried again. This time I didn't sound so loud. It sounded good. Soon I forgot all about where I was and just kept playing "Up and Down" until I had it perfect.

There were thumping noises.

"Time's up!" called a voice, and I was bumped off the piano bench.

"Hide!" Maggie hissed. "It's my dad." I dove behind the couch.

The door opened. "Sounded great," said Maggie's dad. "Didn't I say you'd like it?"

"Yes, Dad," Maggie said.

He went off whistling "Up and Down." I crawled out from behind the couch. "It worked," said Maggie. "All right, what a plan!" We traded high fives, then we snuck outside and spent the afternoon playing hockey in the driveway.

At dinner that night, I pretended I got Maggie's goals and assists at floor hockey. My parents thought I was going to be a superstar. We had chocolate glop for dessert.

In just three weeks, Maggie got seventeen goals and nineteen assists. She started to say floor hockey was too easy, and maybe real hockey would be better. I learned five new songs and began playing the piano with both hands. My teacher said I had the makings of a real musician.

Our parents thought it was the other way around, and everybody was happy. I was always getting chocolate glop.

Then the problem began. Now that Maggie was supposed to be so good at piano, she started to bug me when I was practising. She began standing beside me and fussing every time I made a mistake.

The worst thing was that nobody would ever know I was the one at the piano no matter how well I played. It was no fun at all.

Nothing was fun anymore. Practising the piano wasn't fun. Playing hockey in the driveway wasn't fun because I always lost. Thinking about winter wasn't fun. After a while, even chocolate glop wasn't fun anymore.

Finally, one Monday, right in the middle of practising, I said, "I quit. I don't want to do this anymore."

"You can't quit," said Maggie. "I made a plan. We made a deal."

"I don't care," I said. "I quit."

"Okay, smarty," said Maggie. "See if I help you anymore. Go play hockey yourself."

"See if I care," I said. "Play your own piano," and I went home.

For the next two days, I was so mad at Maggie, I forgot to think about floor hockey. Saturday seemed a long way away. Besides, it felt good not being bossed and not sneaking around. Sneaking really tired me out after a while.

Then, at dinner on Wednesday, my mother said, "We're invited to a block party at Maggie's on Friday night, Cyril. Won't that be nice? Maggie's mother tells me that Maggie is going to give a little concert on the piano. I hear she's doing very well at her lessons."

I nearly choked on my mashed potatoes.

"Are you all right?" asked my dad.

"Uh-huh," I said. I put my napkin up to my face to hide a big grin. There was no way she could get out of this one. Maggie was sunk.

Or was she? She was pretty smart. What if she did get out of it? Then I thought about how much I missed the piano. I should be the one playing on Friday night. Now I might never have a chance to play again.

The telephone rang as I was helping with the dishes. It was Maggie. She tried to sound tough, but I could tell she was scared.

"I wouldn't call you usually, Cyril, since you're a deal-wrecker. But I've decided to give you another chance," she snapped.

"Forget it," I said. "I don't need another chance. You do. I've already heard about Friday."

"Aren't we still partners?" asked Maggie. She didn't sound as mean now.

"Maybe," I said.

"Come on, Cyril, we're best friends." Now Maggie was talking like I was the nicest person in the world.

"It depends," I said. "You'll have to do everything I say."

"What?" she screeched. "No way! You little. . ."

"Okay, 'bye," I said. "See you Friday."

"Wait a sec," Maggie said, very fast. "We can make a deal. If you teach me piano, I'll teach you hockey."

My mom came into the room.

"No," I whispered. "I'll teach you piano, but I get to do my practising, and you have to keep on playing hockey for me."

She was stuck and she knew it. "Okay," she grumbled.

"Good," I said. "We start tomorrow after school." I hung up the phone feeling terrific. The whole thing had been easy.

Things got harder, fast. When I tried to teach her, Maggie complained that piano was boring. She didn't listen at all.

"I don't have to start at the beginning," she said. "Just show me one song for Friday." Then she picked "Mysterious Melody"—the hardest one. It sounded like she was hitting the keys with her feet when she tried it.

"That's enough," I said. "You just can't play the piano."

"Then what am I going to do?" Maggie asked.

"How about putting on a record and pretending to play?" I suggested.

Maggie thought. "I don't think that will work," she said. Then a gleam came into her eyes. "But if we were real partners again, you could play the piano for me."

"Huh?"

"You could wear a disguise," said Maggie. "As long as they can't tell who's playing, they'll think I am." She paused. "And if you do this for me, I'll fix it so you won't have to worry about floor hockey anymore."

"What will you do?" I asked.

"Just trust me," Maggie said. "It'll work."

That sounded pretty good. I did want to play the piano for a bunch of people, and Maggie was going to do something for me.

"Okay," I said. "We're partners, as long as I can help with the disguise."

"Sure," said Maggie. "We'll start as soon as you finish practising, partner."

On Friday night, everyone on Greenapple Street came to Maggie's with barbecues and stuff to eat. We brought hamburgers and chocolate glop. I was so excited I only had one hamburger and saved my glop.

While I was eating, I saw Maggie talking to Mr. Birney, the man who runs Half-Pint Hockey. I hope she knows what she's doing, I thought. I sure don't want to play real hockey. When they stopped talking, Maggie came over to me.

"Disguise time," she said. We went to the basement to get started.

First, Maggie taped two hockey pucks to the bottom of my shoes to make me taller. Then we cut two eye holes in an old bed sheet and put it over my head. On top of that, I put on some glasses with a big nose and a moustache attached to them. Then Maggie got a baseball cap and pulled it down on my head to keep the sheet from moving around.

As we worked, Maggie said, "I told my Mom I was going to wear a costume to go with the song. She thinks I'm dressing up, not disguising. Now, stick out your arms."

I couldn't see very well with all the stuff on my head, so at first I didn't know what she was doing. Then I felt her loading my arms with junky old bracelets.

"Hey! I didn't pick that stuff!" I said.

"Hold still," said Maggie. "We forgot. Disguising your arms and hands is the most important part." Then she put nail polish on me.

"Eeeewwwwww, yuck," I said.

"Ssshhh," she said. "Shake them dry."

I shook. The bracelets clanked and jangled. I felt stupid. Right then I was glad there was a sheet over my head.

Maggie steered me to the laundry room door.

"Now, when everybody goes into the recreation room, you walk in, go to the piano, and play the song. Don't say a word. Then come back to the door, turn around, and take a big bow. Then I'll get you out of hockey and me out of piano. Oh, and if I'm not around later, I'll be out in the driveway."

In the next room, we could hear everybody coming in.

Maggie's mom said, "It's time for me to introduce a mysterious piano player who's going to play a 'Mysterious Melody.'"

Maggie gave me a shove, and I clomped into the room. There was laughing and clapping as I went to the piano. The hockey pucks were really hard to walk on. I had to hold the sheet up, and it twisted around and made it hard to see.

I bumped into a chair and said, "Ow." A hand steadied me. It was my dad's!

"Ow," I said again, trying to sound like Maggie.

My dad stared at me hard, and I clomped away fast.

I got to the piano bench, tugged my sheet up, and climbed on. It took a second to find middle C. I put my fingers on the keys. All the bracelets rattled down my arms and piled up at my wrists. I shook them back. For the first time, I saw that Maggie had painted my fingernails purple.

It got very quiet, and suddenly I got very scared. My hands felt all wet. I wanted to wipe them on the sheet, but I couldn't move. The keys on the piano didn't make any sense at all. I knew I was going to make a mistake. What song was I supposed to play? I couldn't remember anything.

Then a chair creaked right behind me, and I jumped. My fingers hit the keys. I began playing "Mysterious Melody" faster than I'd ever played it before, bracelets jingling and purple fingers flashing.

I played it twice before I remembered it was supposed to end. The next time through I stopped.

Everybody clapped. Someone yelled "Bravo" and whistled.

I slid off the bench while everybody was still clapping and shuffled to the door. My hockey pucks were clomping. My sheet was flapping. My glasses were bouncing, and all those clunky bracelets were jangling. I was just glad it was over.

By the wall, my mom and dad were whispering to each other and looking at me. I got a little nervous.

But everybody kept on clapping, so I slowed down and waved, just like they do on TV. By the time I got to the door, I was so proud I was wishing they could all see who it really was, even if I did look funny.

"Take a bow! Take off the hat, and take a bow!" Maggie whispered from outside the door. I deserved it. I twisted around to face everyone, swept off the baseball cap, and bowed low to the ground.

I felt a tug from behind. The glasses with the nose and moustache tumbled off. The sheet disappeared between my feet. All that was left was me, with bracelets and purple fingernails, wobbling around on two hockey pucks.

"Cyril!" gasped Maggie's parents.

"Cyril!" said the neighbours.

"I thought so!" said my dad.

I whirled around. Maggie and the sheet were gone. I had been tricked, and now I was trapped. I felt my face get very red and bowed to hide it. People laughed and clapped all over again.

"Great playing, Cyril," they said.

"What a cute trick."

"A born performer."

"I bet you're proud of him!"

My parents said they were. I wasn't sure. My parents and Maggie's acted like they knew what was going on all the time, until everybody had gone upstairs.

"Cyril, wherever did you learn to play the piano?" asked my mom.

"I don't know." I squirmed.

"You don't know?" said my dad. I could tell from his voice he didn't believe me. Neither did anyone else.

There was no reason to pretend any longer, so I told them.

"On Saturdays. At community school," I said. "I practised over here."

"You mean that was you playing every day?" asked Maggie's dad. "Then what was Maggie doing all this time?"

"Playing floor hockey," I said. "She has fifty-seven goals and forty-six assists."

Then I told them all about how we had traded. At first they didn't believe me. Then they looked pretty angry. Then they looked like they couldn't choose between laughing and getting mad.

"Where's Maggie now?" asked her mom.

"She told me she'd be in the driveway," I said.

"We're going to talk more about this later, Cyril," said my dad.

We went upstairs. Maggie and Mr. Birney were in the driveway playing hockey. Maggie was wearing a hockey sweater and taking shots on Mr. Birney in goal. A bunch of people were watching them. Maggie took a slapshot and scored. Mr. Birney looked a little red in the face.

"Sign her up," someone said. "First girl in the league."

"I'm going to be," said Maggie, "if my parents let me."

"If she skates as well as she shoots, she'll be fine," said Mr. Birney.

Maggie's mom and dad looked at each other.

"Why don't we all talk it over?" her mom said.

Maggie started taking shots again. My parents whispered behind me. Then my dad leaned over.

"You really want to take piano, do you, Cyril?" he asked.

"Yes, Dad," I said.

"Then your mother and I think that's what you'd better take. Maggie's parents will let you practise here for a while longer. You should be all rested up for your practising, too, because you're going to be skipping TV and going to bed early to make up for some tall tales you've been telling about hockey."

"Yes, Dad. Thanks, Dad." I felt better all of a sudden.

My dad still seemed disappointed, so I said, "At least you won't have to take me to practise at five o'clock in the morning."

"That's true," he said.

Mr. Birney made a big save with his glove. We both clapped.

"Don't you like hockey, Cyril?" my dad asked.

"Sure," I said. "I like to watch it lots. I like to play it sometimes. I just play piano better."

"Maybe you do at that," said my dad.

Maggie looked over. I smiled and nodded. She winked and stickhandled in on Mr. Birney. Maggie's pretty smart, I thought. I just hope she likes getting up at five o'clock in the morning.

Then I went to get my chocolate glop. I felt like I'd earned it.

The Runners

by Allan Ahlberg

We're hopeless at racing,
Me and my friend.
I'm slow at the start,
She's slow at the end.

She has the stitch,
I get sore feet,
And neither one of us
Cares to compete.

But co-operation's
A different case.
You should see us
In the three-legged race!

Dark and Full of Secrets

by Carol Carrick

Early morning mist rose from the pond like steam from a witch's brew. Christopher's father held the canoe steady. Just as Christopher was climbing in, his dog Ben jumped in with him, making the boat rock.

"Ben!" Christopher yelled, pushing the dog out.

"Home, Ben! Go home!" his father ordered, pointing toward the house. Ben slunk away.

"Today will be a scorcher," Christopher's father said as they pushed off. "A good day for swimming."

"I don't like to go in the pond," said Christopher. "There are *things* in there and the bottom is all mucky."

It wasn't that Christopher didn't like swimming. In the ocean the waves rose clear green like glass and, when they broke over him, the sudsy foam made him tingle. But the pond was dark and full of secrets.

Christopher was startled when some lily pads scraped the bottom of the canoe. His father laughed at the look on his face.

"Did you think that was a sea monster?" he asked.

Christopher didn't like being laughed at.

"There *could* be one," he said.

After the paddle was over, Christopher's father went to the store. He came back with a mask and a snorkel for each of them and brought them down to the beach in front of their house.

"You're only afraid of the pond because it's a mystery to you," his father said. "Wait till you see what's down there."

"I'm not afraid. I just don't like it," Christopher grumbled. But he was excited about trying the mask.

His father showed him how to put it on and how to breathe through his mouth with the snorkel. Christopher floated on his stomach to look through the window of the mask. Ahead he could see his father's swimming feet.

Christopher followed. Away from the beach the bottom was muddy. His father motioned to him to be still and lifted a rock. Under it was a crayfish. Christopher reached out to pick it up and the crayfish shot backward.

He was chasing after it when an explosion of water splashed over his back. Then four furry legs churned the water ahead of him. Ben never wanted to be left behind. Christopher stood up and splashed the dog, who was swimming around them in circles.

"I'll *never* find that crayfish now!" Christopher said.

"I'm hungry anyway," his father answered. "Let's have some lunch."

After lunch his father read a newspaper on the porch, but Christopher wanted to hunt for another crayfish. As he waded in, a turtle slipped off a log into the water, making a tiny splash. Maybe he could catch it. Christopher quickly put on the mask and circled the log, but the turtle was gone.

Christopher paddled among the rocks where crayfish might be hiding. Ahead of him a school of tiny fish hung together like the mobile in his classroom. They turned, swam and turned together, as though blown by the breeze.

Farther along shore the pond was deeper, and spooky. Cedar trees had drowned and fallen into the water, sinking like ancient ships.

Christopher almost missed seeing the big bass because it was so still. The fish was resting in the shade of an overhanging tree.

Christopher stopped moving. He even tried to stop breathing. Then, with a delicate sweep of its tail, the bass swam off. Christopher followed with slow strokes until the fish disappeared in the gloom. His heart pounded with excitement. It was one of the biggest fish he had ever seen. Wait till he told his dad!

Now Christopher floated above a meadow of waving plants. He was beginning to feel part of the underwater world. His breath snored through the breathing tube. The ripples rocked his body. Soon Christopher was almost lulled to sleep.

But water had gradually seeped into his mask. When Christopher stood up to empty it, water closed over his head. His feet felt for the bottom. It wasn't there! He had drifted out too far. Frantic, Christopher tried to drain his mask and tread water at the same time, but he kept sinking.

He started to paddle toward shore. Something scratched his foot. Was it the big fish? He gasped in surprise, filling his mouth and his mouthpiece with water so he couldn't breathe.

The mask was fogged up. He couldn't see what was in the water with him. Maybe it was only a floating branch, but Christopher had panicked. He struggled and pulled off the mask, sinking again. He clawed his

way to the surface, panting for air. Now there was water in his eyes.

"Dad!" he called, but the water gurgled in his throat. Then near his ear he heard a loud puffing. It was Ben!

Christopher managed to grab the dog's long tail and hang on. Ben swam away, towing Christopher behind. As soon as he could touch bottom, Christopher let go.

His father was standing by the water's edge. "You shouldn't be out that far alone," he called. But then he teased, "The sea monster might get you."

Christopher had to catch his breath. Water in his throat made him cough and his legs were wobbly. He stretched out on the warm sand as if he would never move again.

Christopher's father was concerned. "Are you okay?" he asked.

"Sure," Christopher answered, but he didn't sound so sure. "I did get out a little too far," he admitted.

But when he remembered all he had seen, he sat up. "Dad, it was great! It was like being a fish myself. And I saw the biggest lake bass in the whole world. I was *that* close." Christopher measured with his hands.

Before sunset, the whole family went for a canoe ride. This time Ben came along.

The pond was like a dark mirror, reflecting puffs of pale cloud. And like a mirror, Christopher couldn't see through it. But beyond that dark surface, he knew there was a crayfish that swam backward, a turtle that liked to sun itself, and a bass that maybe no one else had ever seen.

When the Ships Come in

We go down to the shipyard
when the ships come in.
There's lots to discover, so let's begin!

There's a Shipyard in Marystown

by Clayton Graves

My name is John Hanrahan. Since I was a little kid, I've always loved ships. Now I work at the Marystown Shipyard, where we build and repair all kinds of vessels—tug-boats, fishing trawlers, search and rescue boats, and supply ships. We also build and repair giant floating oil rigs. I'm proud of the work we do here, and when some children from Harfitt Primary School asked if they could come to the Shipyard, I planned a tour I hoped they'd never forget.

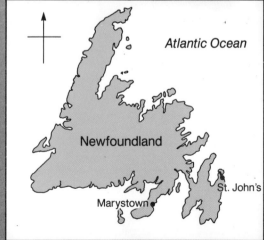

Atlantic Ocean

Newfoundland

St. John's

Marystown

Cory   Judy   John   Stephanie   Bryr

Derek   Nigel   Jennifer   Dion

The Shipyard is a busy place, with lots of machines at work. Everyone who enters must wear a hard hat for safety. When I met the children at the gate, the first thing I did was give each of them a hard hat.

Hull 37 was our first stop. Cory led us up the **gangway** onto the main deck of the ship.

 From Hull 37's upper decks, we had a good view of the whole Shipyard. A special elevator for ships, called a **synchrolift**, had already raised three large vessels out of the water and onto the wharf.

 Stephanie was curious about the ship's watertight doors, so I showed her how they work. To lock the door, you turn the wheel in the middle one full turn. That's important when the ocean is rough and giant-size waves crash all over the ship's deck.

On Hull 37

When I said, "Let's go up to the **bridge**," some of the children looked puzzled. I explained that the bridge is the control centre of a ship. It's on the top deck. From the bridge, the ship's Captain and the First Mate can see clearly in all directions.

➡ Of course, the children wanted to try out the instrument panel with all its dials, knobs, and controls. Bryna decided to play Ship's Captain.

➡ Dion pretended he was making an important call to other ships at sea. Nigel made a call to get the latest marine weather forecast.

Some of the kids were surprised to find out that modern ships like Hull 37 are steered with a **joystick** rather than a wheel.

Jennifer and Stephanie received their orders to start up the engines. Derek called the Harbour Master for permission to leave the harbour.

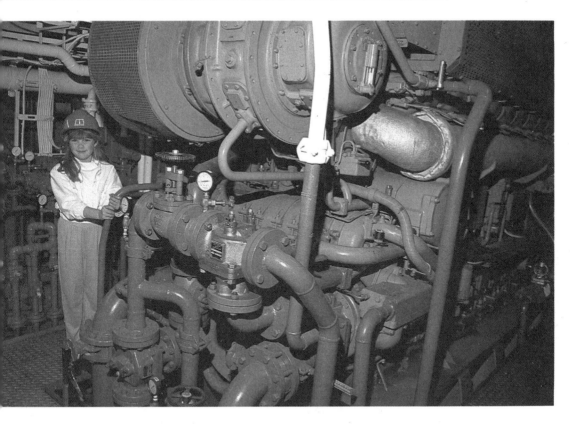

 Bryna gave this engine a good inspection and decided it was ready to go.

 After all this work, it was time for a snack in the ship's **mess**. That's where the crew eats and relaxes. Judy could see her house on shore, through the round **porthole**. She wondered if her brother could see her.

On the Wharf

We left Hull 37 and stepped back onto dry land. *Zebulon*, a fishing trawler, was already up on the wharf, and its repairs were about to start.

There were white crusty barnacles and sea weed growing all over its **hull**, and especially on its **propellers** and **rudder**. This could slow down its speed in the ocean. *Zebulon's* hull had to be cleaned from **bow** to **stern**.

One of the workers cleaned the hull with a high-pressure spray gun. A jet of water knocked the barnacles right off.

A welder found some holes in *Zebulon*'s steel hull. He cut out damaged parts and welded new steel patches over the holes. He wore a safety mask to protect his eyes from the light of the welding torch and from the flying pieces of glowing hot steel.

Our favourite trawler got three new propellers... and a fresh coat of paint.

At the Oil Rig

⬆ Across the bay from Marystown, there's a special shipyard for oil rigs. That is where I took the children next—to see an oil rig that was in for repairs.

The oil rig stands on eight large legs that are anchored to the ocean floor. In each leg there is also an engine and a propeller so the rig can move on its own.

The highest part of the rig is called the **derrick**. There is a landing pad on top so that helicopters can transport workers and supplies to and from the rig.

As the children walked out to the oil rig, they looked like tiny ants.

The children were amazed at the size of the oil rig's anchor chains. Each link is about one metre long.

We talked to some of the engineers who design oil rigs. Their drawings are called **blueprints**. The engineers are planning a new rig that's even bigger than the one we visited.

Hold Onto Your Hats!

Before the children left the Shipyard, I took them to see our newest ship, the *Funk Island Banker.* There was a Name-the-Vessel contest for this ship. Judy knew the children, who go to a school in Garnish, who sent in the winning name.

⬆ The children got another idea of how the Shipyard works when I showed them a tabletop model. Derek said he thought it needed some model ships. Bryna came up with a brilliant idea: "Let's make some model ships when we get back to school!" And I said, "If you're going to be building ships, you'd better keep these hard hats."

Island Hopping

The world is full of islands.
There's a special one for you.
HOP TO IT!

Tropical Trinidad

by Christine McClymont

Maracas Bay

Port of Spain

If you love island hopping,
you'll want to put Trinidad
high on your list.

You can fly there in a few
hours or cruise slowly through
the turquoise waters of the
Caribbean sea. Choose winter
or spring, and you'll have no
hurricanes to worry about.

It's near the Equator there, so
the sun is *hot*. Pack lots of
sunscreen lotion.

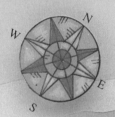

You've arrived in Port of
Spain, and the first sound you
hear is the lilting beat of a
calypso song. This is Trinidad,
home of the steel band.

Run down to the beach at Maracas Bay. If you're lucky, a Trinidadian boy will give you a drink of cool, sweet coconut milk.

Along the beach, fishermen are hauling in a huge net called a seine. Leaping fish sparkle in the sun.

For dinner, munch some "shark and bake" (shark meat in fried bread, seasoned with lots of red peppers). The talk is all about tonight's parade.

It's Carnival Time! People sing and dance all night. And you just might meet a storyteller who'll tell you this tale.

How Trouble Made the Monkey Eat Pepper

by Grace Hallworth

An old woman used to buy molasses from a nearby village. One day, as she was returning home, she tripped over the roots of a tree and her calabash fell and broke, spilling the molasses she had just bought.

When the old woman saw her molasses running on the ground and going to waste, she began to cry.

"Lordie, Lordie, look at mi trouble, oui,
Lordie, Lordie, how trouble overtake me!"

She scooped up as much of the molasses as she could with a bit of broken calabash and continued on her way. As soon as she had gone, Monkey climbed down from the tree where he had seen and heard all that had happened.

He sniffed the treacly, sweet syrup on the ground and in no time he had licked it all up.

"Yum, yum!" he said, smacking his lips. "If this is trouble, then I'll have double." And off he ran to the village shop to buy some trouble.

Now when Monkey entered the shop and asked for double trouble, the shopkeeper could make neither head nor tail of it. So Monkey explained what had happened to the old woman. Then the shopkeeper saw his chance of getting even with Monkey, who had pelted him with coconuts the last time he had taken a shortcut through the forest.

He went to the back of the shop, seized two bulldogs sleeping there, and put them into a sack which he tied securely. Then he returned to the shop and handed the sack to Monkey.

"There's enough trouble in here to keep you busy for quite a while," said the shopkeeper.

Without so much as an "If you please," or a "Thank you," Monkey threw his money down on the counter, grabbed the sack, and rushed off. He ran deep, deep into the forest until he came to a quiet shady patch under a gru-gru palm, where he sat down and made ready to enjoy trouble. No sooner had he opened the sack than the two bulldogs jumped out and rushed to attack him. Monkey barely had time to leap to a branch of the gru-gru palm and there he crouched, not daring to move, the hot sun burning into his skin, and the thorns digging into his paws, and the bulldogs baying and barking at the foot of the tree.

Thus it was that the shopkeeper found Monkey late, late that evening when he went to look for his dogs.

"Ah Monkey! What trouble is this I see?
Double trouble wait under this tree!"
said the shopkeeper.

Poor Monkey was so faint and weak, he could hardly speak. Growing quite near was a pepper tree laden with red-hot peppers. He had eaten nothing all day and peppers, even red-hot peppers, were better than nothing.

Monkey reached out and devoured pepper after pepper until there wasn't a pepper left on the tree.

Tears ran down his face, and as the pepper burned his tongue, his mouth, and his stomach, Monkey gasped.

"I have had my fill of trouble.
Hungry and thirsty, I'm seeing double."

"Then," said the shopkeeper, "take my advice, Monkey, and never trouble trouble unless trouble trouble you."

Beautiful Baffin Island

by Christine McClymont

If you want to beat the summer heat, fly up near the Arctic Circle and visit Canada's largest island.

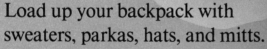

Load up your backpack with sweaters, parkas, hats, and mitts.

When you land in Iqaluit, friendly Inuit people will show you to your hotel. You might find it hard to sleep. In summer, it never gets dark, here in the land of the midnight sun.

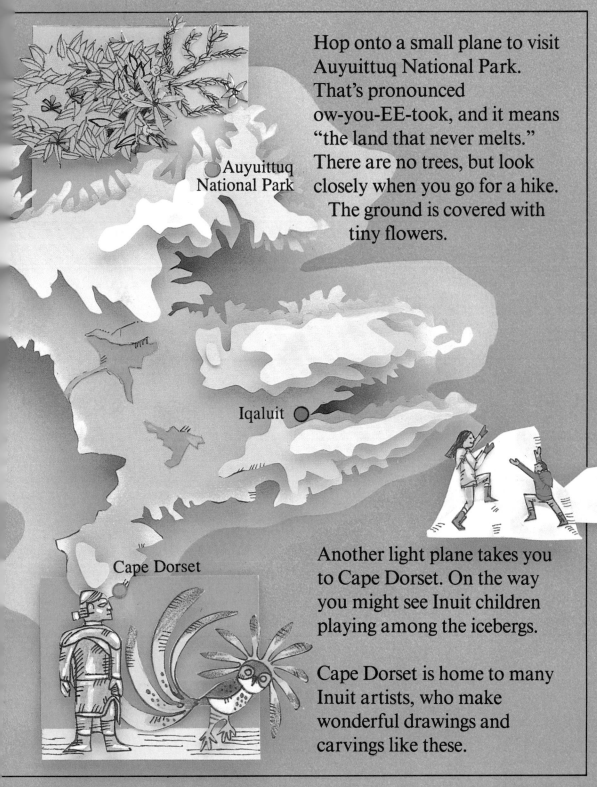

Hop onto a small plane to visit Auyuittuq National Park. That's pronounced ow-you-EE-took, and it means "the land that never melts." There are no trees, but look closely when you go for a hike. The ground is covered with tiny flowers.

Auyuittuq National Park

Iqaluit

Cape Dorset

Another light plane takes you to Cape Dorset. On the way you might see Inuit children playing among the icebergs.

Cape Dorset is home to many Inuit artists, who make wonderful drawings and carvings like these.

Baffin Island Artists *by John McInnes*

Arctic Madonna
Pitaloosie Saila (1942 -   )

Cape Dorset print
Stonecut and stencil

Pitaloosie used the shape of a woman's parka to frame her picture of a mother and child. Pitaloosie never knew her own mother, and was thinking of her when she made the drawing for the print.

Taleelayu and Family   Stencil #30   Ananaisie Alikatuktuk / Ananaisie Alikatuktuk   Pangnirtung   1976

Taleelayu and Family
Ananaisie Alikatuktuk
(1944 -   )

Pangnirtung print
Stencil

Ananaisie made this picture of the sea goddess and her children. The goddess is called Taleelayu. The three female children have scales that look like coats. The males do not have scales. The colours are like the colours under the ice of the Arctic Ocean.

Seal

Ottochie Ashoona
(1942 - 1969)

Cape Dorset carving
Green stone mottled brown

Ottochie carved this seal out
of green stone. This funny
fellow stands upright on his
large rear flippers as if he were
about to dance.

Football Player
Ovilu Tunnillie (1949 -

Cape Dorset carving
Green stone

Ovilu carved this football player after watching football games on television. She had seen athletes getting trophies. She thought a football player would be happy to get a carving such as hers as a trophy. Her husband quarried the stone for the carving.

Spectacular Sicily

by Christine McClymont

Sicily is the largest island in the
Mediterranean Sea. When
you approach it by ferry,
you'll see steep mountains
sloping down to the shore.

A train transports you to
Palermo. If you hear loud
shouts along the narrow
streets, it's the sellers in the
market advertising their fish,
lemons, and eggplant.

When you're hungry, visit a
trattoria (casual restaurant)
for a sword fish and pasta lunch.
And you'll love Sicilian ice cream
and marzipan candy!

Palermo

You might see a puppet show—in Italian—about knights of old.

Don't miss the most exciting adventure in Sicily—the cable car ride up Mount Etna. It's the highest active volcano in Europe.

Taormina

You can see the lava when you peer down the crater at the top. Afterwards, you can relax on the beach of Taormina.

Last stop, Syracuse. Take a seat in the huge semi-circular theatre. It was built by settlers from Greece 2500 years ago!

Syracuse

There is a good story about a Greek boy who won a musical competition in this theatre.

Mt. Etna

Arion and the Dolphins

by Lonzo Anderson

This boy was Arion. He loved to play the lute and sing. He made friends with the dolphins who lived in the sea. He swam and played tag with them. For them he made his music day after day. The dolphins dived and leaped in time with the music, and danced along the tops of waves on the tips of their tails.

Arion lived in Greece, at Corinth, in the palace of the king, long, long ago. The king told him of a musical contest. It was in Sicily, far away. The first prize was all the gold the winner could carry.

"Why, I can win that," said Arion.

Arion sailed to Sicily aboard a ship that had both oars and sail.

Every day he sat on deck practising his music.
The oarsmen listened and sometimes forgot to
row. The sailors listened and forgot the sail. And the
dolphins followed the ship all the way, because Arion
was there.

At Syracuse, a Greek city on the island of Sicily,
Arion came to the musical fair. He played and sang for
a great crowd of people. He won the first prize, all the
gold he could possibly carry.

The ship set sail for home. Arion was on board with his gold.

The sky was crystal clear, blue, blue in the golden sunlight. The wind and the sea did everything to help the ship on its way, and the dolphins were there, escorting it home to Corinth.

The crew forgot about Arion's music and thought only of his gold. Near the end of the homeward voyage, the seamen came to kill Arion for the gold. There were too many of them. He could not fight them all.

"Let me sing one last song," he said quietly.

"That is reasonable," the captain said.

Arion stood in the bow of the ship. He sang as he had never sung before. He played like an angel.

Even the most evil seamen listened with wonder. The birds flew down from the sky, and the creatures of the sea, from far and near, came close to hear his music. And there beside the ship the dolphins swam.

Suddenly Arion leaped overboard. The waves covered Arion. He clung to his lute. Down and down he sank, deep in the blue sea. The dolphins were with him. One offered him a fin. She brought him to the surface before he could drown. He was so far from the ship that the seamen could not see him among the waves.

When the ship was out of sight, Arion climbed on the dolphin's back and rode her like a horse through the waves. The others swam along on all sides, chattering with joy. The dolphins took Arion straight to his homeland, moving faster by far than the ship. When the dolphins delivered him safe and sound on the beach, Arion thanked them with all his heart. The dolphins leaped high in the air to show their pleasure.

In the distance stood the king's palace at Corinth. Arion travelled toward it. Arion entered the palace, and the king came to meet him. When he heard what had happened, the king was furious.

The ship reached the shore. The seamen came to the king to collect their pay.

"But where is Arion?" the king asked in anger.

"He did not return with us," the captain said.

Now Arion stepped out of hiding and faced the seamen.

They fell at his feet, begging for their lives.

The king roared at them, "You shall die! But you will never know when death may strike you, at any hour of the day or night, wherever you may be, whatever you may be doing. Now, bring Arion his gold!"

The seamen obeyed, then ran away in fear.

"Ho-ho-ho! Ha-ha-ha!" the king shouted, slapping his leg in delight.

Arion laughed along with him and said, "And they will never know that no one is going to harm them at all!"

Arion ran down to the seashore and sang to his friends, the dolphins, "Cooee, coohoo, ho-ho-ho! Cooay, cooah, ha-ha-ha!"

The dolphins listened and chattered and danced. They seemed to be laughing, too, as Arion dived in for a swim with them.

Open a Magic Door

Open a magic door
and you'll never be quite the same.

Arnold
of the Ducks

by Mordicai Gerstein

One hot May morning, while
the sheep dog Waldo snoozed in
the shade, little Arnold was
scooped out of his wading pool by
a near-sighted pelican and carried
off.

His mother, who had run into
the house to get him some apple
juice, saw it happen from the
kitchen window. She screamed,
but it was too late.

The pelican gained altitude
and headed for the sea.

It happened so fast, all Arnold
knew was that suddenly it was
dark and smelled of fish. He
started to cry and kick and
scream. The startled pelican did a

double roll and a flip. Arnold tumbled out. They were over the marshes, and Arnold landed in a nest of freshly hatched ducklings.

Mrs. Leda Duck, the mother, had gone off for a few minutes to find some snacks for her new family. When she got back, she was very surprised to find Arnold.

"Were you here before, or are you a late hatcher?" she asked him. "My goodness," she thought, "this is not a good-looking duckling!"

Arnold started to cry. "Mama!" he cried. "Mama, mama!" All the ducklings began to quack and cry also.

"Now, now," said Leda, and fed them all sweet grass, and some baby mosquitoes. They liked that, and quacked for more. Arnold, too.

"Welcome, all of you," said Leda. "Welcome to the wonderful world of ducks!"

Arnold was trained along with his duck brothers.

"First the duck walk," said Leda. "Pay attention, all of you. This is how it's done. Quackstep one, and step quack two, and step one quack...."

"What kind of a duck is that?" Three house sparrows were giggling and pointing at Arnold. "Why, it looks more like a monkey than a duck," they laughed.

"And look!" chirped the littlest one. "It has no feathers!"

"Oh dear," said Leda. "Come children, let's give him some of our extra feathers, and dress him up a bit."

Using mud and marsh slime, they stuck feathers all over Arnold's body. The sparrows thought it was a joke, but they helped, too.

When they were finished, Arnold did look a little more ducklike.

Eventually, he learned to do an acceptable duck walk—though he was better at hopping, which his duck brothers couldn't do at all.

Next, Leda led them right into the marsh.

"Swimming lessons, children," she said. "Quack and paddle, quack and paddle...."

Arnold went right in, and went right under. He swallowed some marsh water the wrong way, he coughed and splashed, but finally he did an acceptable paddle.

It was a dog paddle, but Leda chose to ignore that. She knew he would never be your average duckling, but he tried hard and he was very lovable. In fact, she might have loved him a little more than the others, though she'd never have admitted it.

The surprising thing was how easily Arnold took to flying. Taking off from water is not easy. Even for a duck. Arnold began by kind of hopping along through the shallows and waving his arms. The hops became leaps with a lot of flapping. Then he flew, and he flew well. He liked to rest on the breeze till he saw a fish. Then he'd dive.

Unlike most ducks, Arnold liked to land in trees. It made Leda very nervous.

"Come down from there, dear," she would plead. "You might fall."

The sun rose and set, and the seasons passed quickly. Arnold grew much bigger than his brothers. They kept having to refeather him.

From time to time, a story would appear in the news about someone having seen a huge duck with a short bill. Most people thought it was just another UFO.

In fall, Arnold and his family would fly to Florida to spend the winter. Leda carefully avoided people, and taught her ducklings to avoid them, too.

In Florida, Leda had some relatives that were flamingos. They would paddle around the swamps, fishing and quacking.

One spring, just as they were nearing their home marsh after a long flight, Arnold saw a large, shiny, red-and-silver thing fluttering in front of them.

"What is it?" he asked Leda.

"It's just a kite," she answered, "and it's a people thing, so for goodness' sake, stay away from it!"

But Arnold couldn't stay away from it. Leda didn't see him turn and fly back.

The kite was covered with stars and stripes, and it seemed to dance with him. As he flew around and around it, he began to remember things. Things from another life.

Suddenly the wind changed, and the kite lurched at him. The string wrapped around his arms and legs. He struggled, but the kite went into a dive. He plunged to earth.

Arnold was shaken by his fall, and he'd hurt his shoulder. When he looked up, a huge shaggy sheep dog was standing over him. He and the sheep dog looked at each other. Then the big dog sniffed him all over, which made Arnold giggle. He was ticklish. Then the dog sneezed and very gently picked Arnold up in his huge mouth. He carried him out of the park and through the streets.

"Where are you taking me?" quacked Arnold.

The dog didn't answer. Partly because he didn't understand, and also because his mouth was full of Arnold. Finally he went up the walk of a little white house and scratched at the screen door.

A woman came to the door. It was Arnold's real mother. "My goodness," she said. "What have you brought us today, Waldo?"

Arnold didn't recognize her.

She looked more closely. Arnold was covered with feathers and mud and wrapped up in the remains of the kite.

She didn't recognize him either.

"Whatever it is, it needs a bath," she said.

She and Arnold's father, her husband, put the duck child into a nice hot bubblebath. All the feathers and mud and marsh slime washed away.

"It's Arnold!" screamed his mother, and she fell into the bathtub.

Arnold flew out and flapped around the house, but without his feathers, and all wet, he didn't fly too well.

His father finally caught him in the dining room. His mother and father both cried and hugged him and kissed him. They had looked everywhere for him.

It took several weeks to retrain Arnold from a duck to a human child. They patiently taught him to eat with his "wings," or hands, and not his "bill." Later came spoons and forks and knives. They taught him to speak English, and a few words of Spanish and Yiddish. He told them all about his life as a duck. They were amazed.

At night, tucked into his bed, sometimes he dreamed of his duck mother, Leda, and his duck brothers.

The years passed, and one fall day, as Arnold was on his way to school, he heard a familiar sound. He looked up and saw a family of ducks flying south.

"Mother!! Brothers!! Wait!! It's me!" he shouted. "It's me!"

Leda turned her head, startled. Was it the voice of her long-lost duckling? She looked down, but all she could see was a boy, waving his arms and shouting.

"Just my imagination," she thought, as a tear blew from her eye.

Arnold started to run after them. He had kicked his shoes off, and thrown down his books and jacket, when he stopped. He wasn't a duck. He was a boy. He watched his old friends till they disappeared into the clouds. Then he picked up his things and went on to school.

Caleb and Kate

by William Steig

Caleb the carpenter and Kate the weaver loved each other, but not every single minute. Once in a while they'd differ about this or that and wind up in such a fierce quarrel, you'd never believe they were husband and wife.

During one of those crazy quarrels, Caleb got so angry, he slammed out of the house, hating his wife from top to bottom; and she, for her part, screamed after him the most odious insults that came to her mouth.

Caleb went crashing into the forest by their house, pondering why he had married such a cantankerous

hoddy-doddy; but after he'd walked a while, his fury faded and he couldn't remember what it was they had quarrelled about. He could only remember that he loved her. He could only remember her dimples and her sweet ways, and what fragrant noodle pudding she made.

Instead of going straight back to put his arms around her and kiss her warm neck, he decided, since he was already there, to look in the forest for oak trees he could cut down later and take to the mill. He wandered farther in the woods, grew leg-weary, and, lying down to rest for just a moment, was overcome with all the greenness and slipped into a green sleep.

Before long, the witch Yedida, who lived in a hidden cave in that forest, came shuffling by in her slippers, saying secret spells to herself. She stopped short where Caleb was lying, snoring away like a beehive. "How timely!" she snickered. "Here's my chance to test that new spell Cousin Iggdrazil just taught me."

Squatting down, she touched her skinny thumb to the tip of Caleb's left forefinger and, careful not to wake him, barely wheezed these words:

> *Ammy whammy,*
> *Ibbin bammy,*
> *This is now*
> *A bow-wow-wow.*

And there at her feet, instead of a snoring carpenter, was a snoozing dog. "What a darling spell!" she crowed; and pleased to have worked her day's worth of mischief, the witch departed, swollen with pride.

It was sundown when Caleb woke. First he yawned, then he stretched, then he reached to scratch in his armpit. With his *leg*?! Holy gazoly! His eyes bulged and his big mouth hung open and slavered. Where he should have seen a belt and breeches and a pair of heavy brogans, he beheld the belly and hairy legs of a dog!

He was on his feet in an instant, all four of them. Terrified, he spun around to see what he could see of himself. He couldn't believe what he saw. Of course not! Such things don't happen. Oh no? "This is clearly me," he realized. "I'm not dreaming. I'm a dog!"

"*Now* what?" he wondered. "Well, all I can do is go back and explain what happened." And he began trotting homeward, stunned by his new condition, his tail swinging from side to side. Whatever in the world of wonders was it all about? He was suddenly a dog. True, but he was also Caleb the carpenter. He had Caleb's thoughts. And he was running home to his wife, Kate, wasn't he? Yes, on four legs, and sick at heart.

Night fell and there was a simple moon. Kate, at home, was stumbling from room to room, bumping into furniture, dizzy with dread. She had been at every window again and again, peering out, and had been outside many times, but had seen no part of Caleb.

Had her husband deserted her? she asked herself. No, he loved her; he had said so often. But maybe he was fed up with her. Or maybe something had happened to him, a catastrophe.

Caleb was outside the door just then, reluctant to come in and show himself. He was ashamed of being a dog. But at last he worked up the courage to scratch. When Kate held the door open and he saw her pale, worried face, he scrambled over the sill, thrust his hairy paws up on her apron, and strove to say, "Katie, it's me!" Only a suffering growl escaped his throat. He tried again. And again. He could imagine himself saying "Kate," but couldn't say it.

"Poor, lost animal!" she cried. She gave him some water in a bowl on the floor, and a piece of leftover ham. Caleb drank avidly, but he had no heart to eat.

When Kate put a shawl on her shoulders and started to leave, he knew she was going out to look for him, and tried to stop her. He held her shoe in his teeth.

"Stand aside, silly dog," she scolded. "This is no time for games. I must find my dear husband. He may be in terrible trouble." Caleb let her go and trotted gravely after.

All night they traipsed through the moon-laced forest. There was no finding Caleb because there he was behind his wife, with the shape and the shadow of a dog.

At home again in the cool morning, her shoes wet with dew, weary Kate fell asleep in a chair Caleb had made for her, and the maker slept at her feet.

When they woke at noon, Kate searched again in the forest, with the woebegone Caleb dogging her heels, sniffing the ground for no good reason except that he felt he had to.

Then she went into town and made inquiries there, in the tavern, at the post office, in the shops, on the green. Everyone was deeply concerned and would keep an eye out, but no one had caught even a glimpse of Caleb—coming, going, or standing still.

When Kate went to bed that night, Caleb got into his rightful place beside her, snuggled against her dear body, kissed her sweet neck as he'd always done, and sighed out his sorrows. She welcomed the dog's warmth. With him there, she felt less bereft.

She fell asleep with her arm around him, but he was awake all night, wide-eyed, wondering. How could he manage to make himself known to his wife? If he could only tell her somehow that the dog in her arms was her husband! If he could only return to his natural state. Or if Kate could perhaps become a dog. Then they could be dogs together.

Kate decided to keep Caleb. She bought him a collar studded with brass, and she named him Rufus because his fur was reddish, like her husband's hair. She taught him tricks: to stand on two legs, to sit, to shake hands, to fetch things she asked for, to count by barking, to bow. She could hardly believe how fast he learned.

Whenever their friends came calling, Kate would show off her dog. He enjoyed these gatherings, the human conversation, but he didn't like to have his head patted by his old cronies.

Kate grew to love her dog, very much indeed. But though they gave each other comfort, they were far from happy. Kate longed for her missing husband; she couldn't understand why he'd left her. And how Caleb wished he could speak and explain! He would sprawl by her feet, gnawing a bone, while she worked at her weaving. Often a tear would hang from her lashes, or she would stare through the window and sigh, and Caleb would put his paws in her lap and lick her sad face. Kate would scratch fondly behind his ears, caress his fur, and tell him how lucky she was to have such a faithful friend.

One afternoon in late summer, when Caleb was stretched under a tree revelling in the green smell of the grass, some other dogs turned up and enticed him into a romp. Caleb loved it, but soon quit and retired into the house, where the others dared not follow. He had

discovered that being a dog among dogs could be joyous sport, but he didn't want to forget who he was.

The dogs came by a few times more, but Caleb gave them no encouragement, and they stopped coming.

Months passed, in their proper order. From time to time Caleb was drawn back to the place where he'd turned into a dog. He hoped he might find in that luckless spot some clue to the secret of his transformation. He would lie down where he had fallen asleep that day, pretend to be sleeping again, and watch intently through slitted eyes. Chipmunks scurried about in sudden darts, birds were busy in the branches, leaves bent with the roving breezes, a legion of insects hummed. Grasshoppers, on occasion, catapulted through the air. Caleb saw nothing extraordinary. He tried chewing various plants, on the wild chance that one of them might change him back to a man. No such thing even began to happen.

Winter came; snow fell. It was eight months since Caleb had become a dog. He kept warm near the glowing fireplace, dozing much of the day. He watched Kate move through the house, hopeless now about ever being able to reveal his true self. And what if she did learn who he was? Would it make her happier? Well, she would know that he hadn't deserted her; but would she relish having a dog for a husband? He decided she wouldn't.

One crisp, starry night, long after Christmas, burglars crept up to the warm, sleeping house. They deftly pried open a window and stole into the parlour with a drift of icy air. But Caleb was instantly up and barking. He scurried through the bedroom door straight at the intruders.

"Fry this stupid mongrel!" cried the shorter burglar, trying to fend him off. Caleb locked his jaws on the man's arm. The taller burglar seized Caleb by the collar, but Caleb held fast.

Kate, torn from her dreams by the hubbub, saw her brave dog fighting two men and ran to help. She pummelled the one who had hold of Caleb and pulled his coarse hair. He wheeled and flung her to the floor, hissing broken curses through his beard. That very instant, Caleb rushed him, hoarsely snarling and showing his dangerous fangs. The terrified thief drew a knife from a pocket in his rags and slashed crazily at Caleb, slicing a bit of skin off a toe on his front paw.

A miracle! Caleb didn't yelp with pain. He yelled the word "Ouch!" and holding his injured paw to his mouth, he was astounded to find it a bleeding hand.

The thief had cut the toe that had been the finger through which the witch Yedida had worked her spell, and the spell was undone! Caleb was Caleb again, clad in his old clothes.

"It's me!" he shouted exultantly. Kate gaped, then "Caleb!" she shrieked. The thieves, frightened to the point of insanity, dived through the window and vanished. They ran so fast they left no footprints in the snow.

Caleb and Kate leaped into each other's arms and cleaved together for a long time.

Much later, when they were able to talk intelligently, Caleb told her, or tried to tell her, what had happened— so far as he knew. What had actually happened they never found out. Like many another thing, it remained a mystery.

I Met a Dragon Face to Face

by Jack Prelutsky

I met a dragon face to face
the year when I was ten,
I took a trip to outer space,
I braved a pirates' den,
I wrestled with a wicked troll,
and fought a great white shark,
I trailed a rabbit down a hole,
I hunted for a snark.

I stowed aboard a submarine,
I opened magic doors,
I travelled in a time machine,
and searched for dinosaurs,
I climbed atop a giant's head,
I found a pot of gold,
I did all this in books I read
when I was ten years old.

Project Manager: Jocelyn Van Huyse
Senior Editor: Sharon Jennings
Series Design: Rob McPhail and Lorraine Tuson
Design and Art Direction: Rob McPhail
Cover Illustration: Suzanne Duranceau
Typesetting: Trigraph Inc.
Printing: The Bryant Press Limited

Acknowledgements
Permission to reprint copyrighted material is gratefully acknowledged. Information that will enable the publisher to rectify any error or omission will be welcomed.

Better Together: Originally titled "Together" from EMBRACE: SELECTED LOVE POEMS by Paul Engle. Copyright © 1969 by Paul Engle. Reprinted by permission of Random House, Inc.

Hockey Stuck: Text copyright © 1986 by Ted Staunton, reprinted with the permission of the publisher, Kids Can Press Ltd., Toronto, Canada.

The Runners from PLEASE MRS. BUTLER by Allan Ahlberg (Kestrel Books, 1983), copyright © Allan Ahlberg, 1983, p. 68.

Dark and Full of Secrets by Carol and Donald Carrick. Text copyright © 1984 by Carol Carrick. Illustrations copyright © 1984 by Donald Carrick. Reprinted by permission of Clarion Books/Ticknor & Fields, a Houghton Mifflin Company.

How Trouble Made the Monkey Eat Pepper from LISTEN TO THIS STORY by Grace Hallworth. Reprinted by permission of Methuen Children's Books, Ltd.

Baffin Island Artists from ARCTIC VISION: ART OF THE CANADIAN INUIT by Barbara Lipton. Copyright © 1984 Canadian Arctic Producers. Used with permission of the publishers.

Arion and the Dolphins: Lonzo Anderson, text of ARION AND THE DOLPHINS. Copyright © 1978 John L. Anderson. Reprinted with the permission of Charles Scribner's Sons, a division of Macmillan Inc.

Arnold of the Ducks: Complete text and illustrations by Mordicai Gerstein. Copyright © 1983 by Mordicai Gerstein. Reprinted by permission of Harper & Row, Publishers.

Caleb and Kate by William Steig. Copyright © 1977 by William Steig. Reprinted by permission of Farrar Straus & Giroux, Inc.

I Met a Dragon Face to Face by Jack Prelutsky reprinted by permission of G. P. Putnam's Sons from ONCE UPON A TIME, copyright © 1986 by G. P. Putnam's Sons.

Illustrations
Donald Carrick: 24-32; Mark Craig: 48-49, 56-57, 62-63; Sharon Foster: 94-95; Marie-Louise Gay: 6-22; Mordicai Gerstein: 72-81; Sandy Hemsworth: 34 (map); Christina Luck: 50-55; San Murata: 5, 33, 47, 71; William Steig: 82-93; Lorraine Tuson: 64-70

Photographs
Barbara Lipton: 58, 61; Jeremy Jones: 23, 48, 56, 62; Peter Strahlendorf, photograph courtesy of Dept. of Economic Development and Tourism, Government of the North West Territories: 59; George Swinson: 60; Ross Tilley: 34-46

34567890 BP 7654321098